3—
can

Mud Pies
and Other Recipes

MUD PIES

AND OTHER RECIPES

A Cookbook for Dolls

MARJORIE WINSLOW

Illustrated by Erik Blegvad

Walker and Company
New York

Text copyright © 1961 by Marjorie Winslow
Illustrations copyright © 1961 by Erik Blegvad

Published by The Macmillan Company in 1961; published
by Pebble Press in 1983. First published in
paperback in 1996 by Walker Publishing Company, Inc.

Published simultaneously in Canada by Thomas Allen & Son Canada,
Limited, Markham, Ontario

Library of Congress Cataloging-in-Publication data
Winslow, Marjorie.
Mud pies and other recipes: a cookbook for dolls/Marjorie
Winslow; illustrated by Erik Blegvad.
p. cm.
Summary: Presents playful recipes for such dishes as "Wood Chip
Dip," "Seesaw Salad," "Roast Rocks," and "Pencil Sharpener Pudding,"
to be prepared for and enjoyed by dolls.
ISBN 0-8027-7487-3 (pbk.)
[1. Cookery—Fiction.]   I. Blegvad, Erik, ill.   II. Title.
PZ7.W7517Mu 1996
[Fic]—dc20   96-19049
CIP   AC

Printed in the United States of America

8   10   9

To Susan and Kate, former
doll chefs, who knew better
than to taste for seasoning
and, therefore, grew up

Contents

FOREWORD

This is a cookbook for dolls. It is written for kind climates and summertime.

It is an outdoor cookbook, because dolls dote on mud, when properly prepared. They love the crunch of pine needles and the sweet feel of seaweed on the tongue. The market place, then, will be a forest or a sand dune or your own back yard.

You can use a tree stump for a counter. The sea makes a nice sink; so does a puddle at the end of a hose. For a stove there is the sun, or a flat stone. And ovens are everywhere. You'll find them under bushes, in sandboxes or behind trees.

Cooking utensils should, whenever possible, be made from something that would otherwise be thrown away. Cutting the side from an empty milk carton leaves a perfect loaf pan, while slicing an inch or two from the bottom of another carton makes a good square cake pan. The bottom half of a heavy cardboard egg carton does nicely as a muffin tin and as a mold for individual cakes and pies. Empty frozen pie pans are very useful. So are frozen orange juice cans, cupped milk bottle tops, small flower pots, pop bottle caps and coffee cans.

Doll cookery is not a very exacting art. The time it takes to cook a casserole depends upon how long your dolls are able to sit at table without falling over. And if a recipe calls for a cupful of something, you can use a measuring cup or a teacup or a buttercup. It doesn't much matter. What does matter is that you select the best ingredients available, set a fine table, and serve with style.

ASSORTED HORS D'OEUVRES

Take the cardboard from a freshly laundered shirt. To this cardboard glue 8 paper baking cups, in pretty colors if possible. This is the hors d'oeuvres tray. Into each cup place anything that comes to mind. Here are 8 examples:

grass	flower petals
clover	crushed dry leaves
pine needles	minced twigs
small berries	gravel

STUFFED SEA SHELLS

Scoop up a shovelful of sand that has just been licked by a wave. Pack this into the tiniest sea shells you can find. Sprinkle these with a pinch of dry sparkling sand and serve.

DAISY DIP

Pick 4 daisies. Remove the stems. Place each daisy in the center of a plate, and surround with 6 or more buttercups, also without stems. Suggest to your doll and her 3 guests that they pull off one petal at a time, dipping in a buttercup before eating.

WOOD CHIP DIP

In a little bowl mix dirt with water until it is as thick as paste. Place this bowl on a platter surrounded by wood shavings. Scoop the dip with the chip.

BERRY BOATS

Pick a middle-sized rhododendron leaf and turn the underneath side up. This forms a little green boat. Now pick the tiny berries, in all colors, that grow on bushes and sometimes on trees. Fill the boat about half full with the berries and serve. This fruit cup also makes a nice fruit salad on a hot day.

SOUPS, SALADS

& SANDWICHES

BOILED BUTTONS

This is a hot soup that is simple but simply delicious. Place a handful of buttons in a saucepan half filled with water. Add a pinch of white sand and dust, 2 fruit tree leaves and a blade of grass for each button. Simmer on a hot rock for a few minutes to bring out the flavor. Ladle into bowls.

MARIGOLD MADNESS

Shred several marigolds into a pan and fill with water. Set in the sun to simmer. When the liquid has turned to gold, strain into bowls and put in the shade to cool. Serve chilled.

MUD PUDDLE SOUP

Find a mud puddle after a rainstorm and seat your dolls around it. Serve.

MOCK MUD PUDDLE SOUP

For dolls who live in a dry climate: Scoop out a little trough in the dirt and run the hose into it for a minute. This kind needs a little seasoning, so add a pinch of the dirt that you dug out. Seat your dolls around the mock puddle and serve.

MOLDED MOSS SALAD

Find a patch of moss. Carefully dig up a flat sheet of it and place on a cutting board. Cut the moss into interesting shapes with cookie cutters, placing each on a leaf. Arrange on a serving platter or place on individual salad plates.

TOSSED LEAVES

Gather enough green leaves to fill a big bowl. Sprinkle with white sand and freshly ground dust, season with minced grass, moisten with a few squirts of water from a squirt gun. Toss it as high as you can with wooden spoons or hands, always making sure the salad returns to the bowl after each toss. When seasonings and leaves are well blended, the salad is ready to serve.

SEESAW SALAD

Follow the recipe for Tossed Leaves, but add the following: a pinch of crushed dry leaves, a fistful each of pine needles and red berries, and two fistfuls of little pine cones. Sprinkle over all a generous amount of sawdust, then turn the hose nozzle to a fine spray and wave it twice over the bowl. Arrange yourself on a seesaw with the bowl in front of you and a friend at the other end. Toss the salad this way as long as it's fun, or until well blended. Serve on large plates.

SANDWICH

The most basic of all sandwiches, of course, is the *sand*wich. This popular food takes many forms. Here are 4 examples:

BEACH SANDWICH Gather some of the broad flat amber leaves of seaweed or kelp. Spread half of each leaf with wet sand and fold.

SANDBOX SANDWICH Mix sand with water in a pail. Spread a thin layer of this mixture on an English ivy leaf. Top with another ivy leaf and serve.

DESERT SANDWICH The sands of the desert have a unique flavor, but there is seldom anything handy to complete the sandwich. Open your doll's hand out wide, palm side up. Sift this dry sand onto the hand. This is an open-faced sandwich and can be licked.

QUICKSANDWICH This filling is hard to find, hazardous to collect and therefore a rare delicacy. Spread between two small skimming stones. Serve quickly.

FRIED WATER

Melt one ice cube in a skillet by placing it in the sun. When melted, add 1 cup water and sauté slowly — until water is transparent. Serve small portions, because this dish is rich as well as mouth-watering.

GRAVEL EN CASSEROLE

Fill individual casseroles with gravel. Brush with melted ice cube, sprinkle generously with crushed dry leaves and bake uncovered in a moderate oven until bumpy on top.

ROAST ROCKS

Place 6 medium-size rocks in an oven and roast until hard on the outside but still rare inside. This takes about as long as chasing a butterfly. Roast Rocks tend to be difficult to slice, so serve each doll a whole rock. Serves 6.

DANDELION SOUFFLÉ

After the dandelions in your lawn have gone to seed, shake their fluffy tops into an empty frozen pie pan until it is brimming over. Set in a moderate oven that is out of the wind. While it is cooking, seat your doll at a table located in a light breeze. Serve the *soufflé* immediately, and just watch it disappear! You will never have leftovers with this dish.

LEAVES EN BROCHETTE

Using a pencil for a skewer, spear as many different leaves as you can find. Alternate the kinds and, if possible, the colors. In a sunny place, rest the skewer on two forked sticks so that it can be turned occasionally in the sun. This is a particularly tasty dish in the autumn.

SILKY SPAGHETTI

Collect enough corn silk to fill a big bowl. Add 2 cups of fresh air and leave in the sun until just tender. If a sauce is desired, the following may be poured over each serving: to 1 melted ice cube, add 1 teaspoon of minced grass and a dash of white sand.

EXCELSIOR & MUD BALLS

Mold some firm mud, mixed with a little dry grass or hay, into balls and place in the sun to bake. When they are hard, serve on a generous nest of excelsior.

CRABGRASS GUMBO

Fill a big pot about half full of hose water. Put in an armload of crabgrass that has been pulled up by the roots from your lawn. Add any other weeds, roots and all, that live in your lawn such as: buckhorn, pigweed, plantain, chickweed. Season with white sand and lots of brick dust.

LEFT-HANDED MUDLOAF

 S it on the ground with a bowl in front of
you full of thick mud. With your left hand,
reach out and add a fistful of whatever
you find there. Stir and pack into a loaf
pan. Mold with left hand.

RIGHT-HANDED MUDLOAF

 F ollow the recipe for Left-Handed Mud-
loaf, but this time use your right hand.

PINE NEEDLE

UPSIDE-DOWN CAKE

Using the square cake pan, cover the bottom with a layer of pine needles. Then mix moist earth from the foot of a pine tree with pine needles and pack the mixture tightly into the pan on top of the layer of pine needles. Place in a hot sun to bake, turning upside down to unmold.

PENCIL SHARPENER PUDDING

Pour the contents of a pencil sharpener into a bowl. Add enough puddle water to soften and stir with a sharp pencil. Allow to set in the shade, either in the bowl or in individual dishes.

PUTTY FOURS

If plumbers or painters are working in your neighborhood, ask them for some putty—enough to fill four acorn cups. These delicate cakes may take days to harden, so plan your party well ahead. Serves 4.

INSTANT MUD CUSTARD

Hurry out after a rainstorm and spoon mud into custard cups.

DOLLYPOPS

Pick a dandelion from the lawn carefully, so as not to disturb the fluff. Hand it to your doll and tell her to lick.

CHALK SHAKE

Grind up one piece of chalk and put the powder into a small shaker. Fill about ¾ full with spring water. If this is not available, cool clear tap water will do. Shake vigorously. Serve at once in the shaker.

BARK SANDWICH

Make a buttery mixture of dirt, lake water and pine needles. Heap this on a piece of birch bark and serve.

GRILLED MUD SANDWICH

Spread mud between two slices of cardboard or two old playing cards. Place on a hot flat stone or sidewalk in the sun to grill.

HOT DOGWOOD

Pick a flower from a dogwood tree. Remove the petals and place them on a flat pan or rock. In each petal wrap a long green pine cone and secure with a toothpick. Broil in the sun.

BACK YARD STEW

Mark off a big square in your back yard by walking 8 giant steps in each direction. Into a large stewpot put anything you find in this square such as grass, leaves, stones, twigs, berries, flowers, weeds and so forth. Season generously with white sand and dust, and add puddle water to cover. The longer this dish stews the better it is.

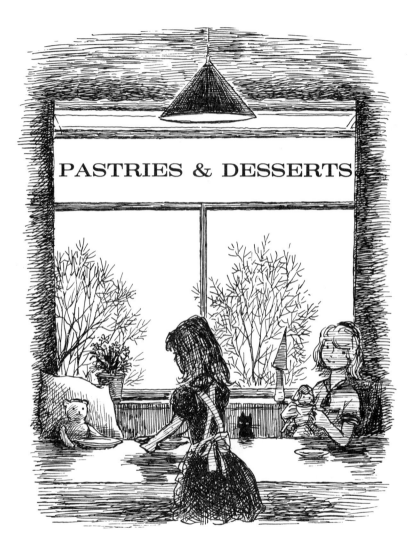

MUD PIES

To a coffee can filled ¾ full of rich dirt, add just enough water to make a very firm mud. Pack this mud into the cups in the bottom half of a heavy cardboard egg carton. Set in the sun to dry slightly, then turn the carton over and unmold on a sunny terrace or sidewalk. When the pies are hard, they are done. Serves 12.

These mud pies keep indefinitely and are good to have on hand for impromptu entertaining.

MUD PIES À LA MUD

Follow the recipe for Mud Pies. Scoop one spoonful of cool moist mud from a shady place onto each pie. Or add a little ice water to some dirt until it is just moist. Put one scoop on each pie.

PIE-THROWING PIES

Follow the first step in making Mud Pies, only make it gloppier. Throw.

EASY AS PIES

In the autumn when the maple leaves have flamed and fallen, choose a large one and cut it into pie-shaped pieces.

SAWDUST CAKE

Mix a little of the clay found along river-banks with sawdust and pack into a square cake pan. Sprinkle with water from a sprinkling can. Bake in the sun until hard, then turn out of the pan and frost with moss.

RAINSPOUT TEA

Place a teapot, or sandpail, at the end of a rainspout and wait for it to rain. After the sun comes out, serve this tea under a rainbow with sawdust cakes or putty fours.

HONEYSUCKLE WINE

Put a honeysuckle blossom beside each plate. They should be slightly chilled in the shade before serving.

MUMS '61

Shred several small or one large chrysan-
themum into a watering can half filled
with hose water. Set in the sun to distill.
The longer this beverage is allowed to
stand, the mellower it becomes. Strain
through the watering can into punch cups.

SUGGESTED MENUS

SUMMER LUNCHEON

Daisy Dip
Marigold Madness
Dandelion *Soufflé*
Tossed Leaves
Putty Fours
Iced Rainspout Tea

BUFFET DINNER

Stuffed Sea Shells
Seesaw Salad
Gravel en Casserole
Excelsior & Mud Balls
Pine Needle Upside-Down Cake
Honeysuckle Wine

WEDDING BANQUET

Assorted Hors d'Oeuvres
Boiled Buttons
Leaves en Brochette
Roast Rocks
Molded Moss Salad
Mud Pies à la Mud
Mums '61

PICNIC

Berry Boats
*Sand*wiches
Hot Dogwoods
Chalk Shakes
Dollypops